THE ULTIMATE GUIDE TO SELF-CARE

THE ULTIMATE GUIDE TO SELF-CARE

Nurture Your Mind, Body, and Soul

B. VINCENT

QuillQuest Publishers

CONTENTS

CHAPTER 1

Introduction

In this fast-paced life, I have found that self-care is a critical prerequisite without which I cannot run any real marathon; it is the foundation of my mental health and provides me with a sense of fulfillment. And when I nurture my mind, body, emotions, and spirit, I flourish. Making time for yourself might seem like a luxury in our always-on world, yet it is essential to creating the life you really want to live. Furthermore, self-care nourishes and sustains our lives and our relationships. It is a paradox in taking care of ourselves so that we can take care of others; we must care first for ourselves. We all have busy lives, yet we need to be aware that our personal well-being is essential if we are to function adequately in the world, childbearing families, and the media who depend on us.

When you think about self-care, what comes to mind? In this hustle-bustle world filled with go-go-go stress and anxiety and overwhelm, self-care has become quite the buzzword. We know that caring for ourselves is essential to living a balanced, joyful life. Still, what does self-care really mean, and how do we implement it? To me, self-care is grounded in stepping back from daily stress and activities long enough to take time for ourselves – to love ourselves and nourish our integrity, rejuvenate our exhausted bodies and tired minds, and connect with the spiritual meaning and values that nurture our souls. Yet the challenge is in finding the time for self-care. Won't taking time for ourselves mean even less time for everything else? On the contrary. With the vitality of self-care, whether physical, emotional, mental, spiritual, or social, you will be more flexible in handling what life throws your way. Just as we support others, we must support ourselves first in the same way.

CHAPTER 2

Taking Care of Your Mind

Make it a habit to set a timer on your phone to remind yourself to take a mental break. Start out with, for example, just a one-minute thought break. I have mine set for eleven times during the day. When it goes off, my mind gets to take a one-minute break. A mindful excursion: pick a place in your yard to focus on for a moment. Maybe a beautiful blossom or a corner of the yard you've been meaning to rediscover. Let your mind go to the discarded cedar swing and how to repair it or the reasons that by season's end, how the yard needs a complete renovation. The more into detail you delve, the more interest you can develop in experiencing it. Take a deep breath! Close your eyes and take three big breaths, clearing your mind of the normal mental background noise. If you are in a quiet place, it's a snap to think the following. If you are in a totally noisy place, it may take a little more concentration, but give it a try. Focus on taking in things around you that need your attention. Take the time to think about each thing; there's a rhythm and a flow to adolescent concept.

Taking care of your mind: when you think about self-care, do you remember to nurture your mind as well as your body and soul? This may be the most often overlooked part of self-care. As with your body, small things can make a difference. Negative mind tape, complain-y thoughts, comparing yourself to others. How can you break the negative tape? Most of us have a running narrative of how bad things are. Let's look at some ways to cut that negative monologue off. Then let's stop complaining to everyone who will listen about how the negative things keep happening. And then, of course, you know at least one person who brags or is just plain sarcastic. Don't go down that road, either. Get off the roller coaster: if you find your mind going to the same negative thoughts time and time again, out of habit, try to find something else to think about.

2.1. Practicing Mindfulness

The habit of meditation or focusing on the present is one that enriches our lives on a myriad of levels. As author Tim Ferriss says, "Regular meditation—say, 5 to 20 minutes per day—allows you to observe your thoughts as if you are an outside observer looking inward. Simply observe your thoughts, name them if you wish, and let them pass by like clouds. This decrease is overidentification with one's thoughts..." Meditation has a number of well-documented physical, psychological, and academic benefits. Setting a fixed time every day—either right after work or school or before bed or after waking up—enables us to create dedicated "down time" as we train our brains toward a state of pure consciousness.

Mindfulness is the practice of maintaining a nonjudgmental state of heightened or complete awareness of one's thoughts, emotions, or experiences. This is an effective way to nurture one's spirit because nurturing your spirituality involves not just going to church on Sundays (or the equivalent in your faith) but building habits that sustain your connection to God, higher power, spirit, or the universe on a daily basis. Building habits of mindfulness maintain our awareness of the miracles in our daily lives, as well as help us stay conscious of how we treat others, including when we are most challenged.

2.2. Engaging in Creative Activities

Dancing, drawing, and discussing artwork that has already been made were all linked to reductions in symptoms of depression, anxiety, and stress for participants in the arts-and-crafts group. Immersing oneself in creative exploration and expression can support overall well-being, bringing emotional grounding, psychological healing, social connection, sensory exploration, and spiritual grounding. To get the best benefit from this skill, start small and keep it simple. Look for inspiration in arts and craft stores, at-home craft kits, or virtually with craft sessions on YouTube. Draw, doodle, paint, or craft without focusing so much on the outcome. This moment in time is for self-expression and curiosity; the finished product is secondary. Some enjoy using coloring books created for meditation practices, as the repetitive motion of coloring helps reduce stress, anxiety, and the other challenges associated with difficult times. After finding a creative activity that fits, carve out dedicated time once a week to add it to the self-care repertoire. Build it up slowly, and then share experiences and creations with friends, family, or online like-minded people in the virtual world.

Creative expression is at the heart of authentic self-care. For millions of patients around the world, art therapy is a tool for healing the mind, body, and spirit. Creativity is linked to the emotional center of the brain. Engaging in creative activities can help unlock emotions, overcome grief, reduce anxiety, and improve mood. Participating in visual arts encourages increased psychological awareness and a healthy flow of self-expression.

CHAPTER 3

Nurturing Your Body

Daily sun exposure, sufficient sleep, and regular exercise are also key to nurturing the body for optimal health, wellness, and disease prevention. According to the National Sleep Foundation, our body's circadian rhythms help determine our proper bedtime. The human body spending so much time indoors and artificially lit by the electrical company can create imbalances in your circadian rhythms. Your body's response to natural sunlight is to stay awake and alert. It is the suppression of an individual's melatonin that is the sleep-wake marker. Melatonin is released from the pineal gland located within the brain. When the sun goes down and darkness falls, perhaps enough of your body's melatonin is being produced, and this begins to make your eyelids grow heavy. While the question of how much melatonin is and should be produced has yet to be determined, it's sparked scientific waiting.

The best way to protect yourself from skin cancer is to avoid direct sun exposure during peak hours of sunlight; use sunblock and wear a hat, sunglasses, and clothing to protect your skin whenever you must be in direct sunlight; seek daily exposure to indirect sunlight, twice that typically recommended by the medical community, during non-peak hours; after sensible sun exposure, shower with soap to avoid fragrance in addition to the sunblock and to remove any film; and conduct regular skin reviews for skin cancer signs/symptoms.

There are more ways to nurture the body and optimize health than may be apparent. Some of the more obvious and common include a well-balanced diet, regular exercise, reserving time each day for relaxation, and getting sufficient sleep. Additionally, one must protect oneself from unnecessary toxins and practice good hygiene by keeping the body clean and well-groomed. Other ways to nurture the body that might not be as common include daily sun exposure and regular surveillance for warning signs of skin cancer.

3.1. Maintaining a Healthy Diet

Although creating a healthy diet plan is challenging, it holds a significant amount of importance when speaking of self-care. When we eat healthily, our bodies are able to heal faster. We also lose and help to maintain our weight when we eat well. Never eliminate your favorite foods from your diet plan. Allow yourself to indulge in treats occasionally. If you do not allow yourself the occasional treats, you are less likely to stick to them, and your cravings for these foods continue to grow. The time will come when you cannot control the cravings, which can often cause binges or giving up on your goals completely. Include a female-friendly diet plan where the calories are stretched out throughout the day. The absolute minimum for a female's diet plan should be 1,500 calories. Anything below this can lead to unhealthy eating habits.

Maintaining a healthy diet is a key part of self-care. When we eat well, we feel well. Processed and fatty foods can slow down your brain function, while nutrient-dense, clean foods can improve how your brain operates. Eating enough is just as important. A diet too low in calories can leave your brain foggy and your body feeling fatigued. Your normal diet should be packed with proteins, like yogurt, cheese, lean meats, and nuts. It should also contain energy-boosting carbohydrates, like fruits, pasta, bread, and cereal. Also, wash everything down with plenty of water. Severe dehydration can make you dizzy, confused, and fatigued. A 2018 study found that drinking a mere milliliter of water for each calorie you eat can help maintain overall health and jump-start weight loss.

3.2. Incorporating Exercise into Your Routine

How much is enough? Begin by approaching the exercise prescription with reasonableness. Entire books are written on the subject, but this guide will keep it simple. The United States Department of Health and Human Service's Physical Activity Guidelines for Americans avow that regular physical activity is one of the most important things people can do to help maintain a lifetime of independent movement and good health. The guidelines recommend a mix of moderate and vigorous aerobic activity each week. It also recommends muscle- and bone-strengthening activities over the course of a week. The following guidelines consider the absolute minimum exercise to maintain overall health benefits for the population, not for an individual wanting to achieve specific outcomes. For those persons just beginning exercise as part of a routine, it is important to "know before you go." A discussion with a physician or qualified health provider can help in determining when to begin a routine, specifically what type of activity is appropriate, how much is recommended, and the types of activities that are, and are not, appropriate. Careful counsel from a professional can help in deciding how often exercises should be performed, how long each exercise session should last, and the degree of strength or physical intensity of the activity that creates improvement. Particular emphasis should be given to experiencing mastery within the physical limits inherent in the activities that help individuals feel powerful and confident at the end of the exercise.

As with any self-improvement strategy, including exercise as a form of self-care requires acknowledgment and commitment. Acknowledgment equates to recognition of the mind and body's inherent need to move and expend energy, and commitment is about cultivating a plan for designing a daily routine that incorporates ample opportunities for physical activity. Achieving this daily balance means integrating strength, flexibility, and endurance exercises that can be tailored to the different levels of ability and different needs of the body and mind. To reach peak self-care capacities, it is important to remember that the entire being is made up of three main components: spirit, mind, and body. Exercise that targets the whole person, while restrained by the power-wielder's current abilities, energy levels, and enthusiasms, results in a happier, more energetic, and more motivated individual.

3.3. Getting Enough Sleep

Give yourself permission. Give yourself permission to do what you need to do to recharge. If that means an annual vacation, a long weekend, or a day to yourself, make it happen. Give yourself a break; don't feel guilty if you'd rather take a day off and read a book than clean the house. There is nothing selfish about caring for yourself. In fact, one of the kinder things you can do is be kind to yourself. That can include taking some time to take care of your own needs. You might also want to add some hobbies and interests to this list. Hobbies are another way to lower levels of stress and leave you feeling relaxed and happy. It's easy to get lost in the everyday hustle, but doing things you enjoy are important. They have a positive effect on our emotional health and help you to fight off feelings of self-doubt.

Getting enough sleep. Be sure to ask yourself, are you getting at least eight hours of sleep? If not, here are some tips for a better night's sleep. About an hour before bed, stop using any electronics like a phone or computer. The blue light that these emit can disrupt your body's natural production of melatonin, a hormone that regulates sleep. Avoid drinks that have caffeine, like coffee or cola, in the afternoon and evening. Caffeine, a stimulant found in coffee, can take eight or more hours to wear off after you drink it, so having a latte or an energy drink, even in the afternoon, can keep you awake. To set the stage for a relaxing night's sleep, follow the same routine every night before bed. Your body will learn that this routine means sleep is on the way.

CHAPTER 4

Cultivating Your Soul

No matter what it is or how it may change over time, it's important to establish what your very own soul medicine is. Incorporate it into your daily life. Better yet, allow it to seep into the conversation in a way that makes it a special, important part of your story. In doing so, you remind others to do it as well. We are, after all, the company we keep. Being yourself is the most powerful thing you can do. Your becoming helps others become. You are contributing to the wellness of those around you when you decide to be yourself. You are influencing others. You are caring for yourself in a way that supports and uplifts others. You are nurturing your own soul.

Before we open our eyes to a new day, before we start thinking about running shoes or making green smoothies or practicing behind-the-scenes social distancing, we can meditate. If these tips feel unconventional in the era of wellness influencers and minimalism branding, it's because they are. Cultivating your soul isn't a performance. It's not a competitive ritual. It's not a status symbol. Nurturing the soul is important because what is important isn't tangible. Much of it is silent. So find the energy for it in the places you might expect. Self-health is grueling and messy work. And if you're doing it well, yes, it should be exhausting sometimes. Here are a few sources of energy to steer you.

4.1. Finding Meaning and Purpose

No two snowflakes are alike. They say the reason is because every snowflake takes a different path to the ground; some are blown by the wind, some start to fall and then are halted by a wind current, and others start falling but are windblown into a new path. So while at first glance snowflakes appear alike, on closer inspection we see they are not. No two people are alike for the same reasons. We all started with the same genetic material, and from there our lives took very different paths. Every day, you are making decisions and setting intentions and recalibrating because of the choices you've made. These are pathways unique only to you. Your life choices have given you a uniqueness that no one else can match. Even identical twins, who share 100 percent of the same DNA, have different life journeys, so the paths they have taken make them unique.

Everyone will experience a time when the answers to these questions are not clear or are impossible to answer. Just because you do not yet have what you perceive as a purpose does not mean that it doesn't exist. You are alive, your heart is beating, you are breathing, so by opening your eyes in the morning, you have purpose. The meaning of your existence may be as simple as breathing in and breathing out. To add value to the world, love yourself and others. You are likely more of an example of light and love than you can imagine. Don't question it; just know it and be it.

4.2. Connecting with Nature

Grounding is a spiritual approach that allows you to connect with the earth and create harmony. It helps you to stay focused and feel both emotionally and physically stable. With your feet planted on the ground, you ascertain a firm bond with the earth and allow the negative energy stuck in your body to escape through the feet. Nature can play a significant role in your life, primarily in your depression treatment, helping you alleviate feelings of anxiety and depression. Walking in the park or some forest and taking the time to sit silently, feel, listen, and look around, and to appreciate all that nature has to offer is an excellent way to relieve the symptoms of depression.

One of the most basic ways to ground and connect, nature nourishes the soul and rejuvenates the spirit. Because of our modern lifestyles, most of us don't spend nearly enough time outside, somewhere that is unspoiled by buildings, cars, and other aspects of urban life, that is quiet and provides a refuge from the bustle of the city. But in fact, we all need to schedule regular time out in nature to ground and center ourselves. Even if you live in a city, you can access beautiful open space without much trouble. If it's not near your work, make a point of visiting a local park or reserve with walking trails on the weekend, and take advantage of the beauty and relaxation that is there for you.

4.3. Engaging in Spiritual Practices

Commune with others. Your religious structure can support the wishes and dreams of their congregation in different ways. Take part in those that nourish your spirit. Remember that all human beings are your sisters and brothers. Show them the same love and kindness that you show those closest to you. Early man prayed to the stars and the heavens for strength. Tapping into this spiritual strength only involves sitting for a moment looking up to the sky. Use this as a way to mentally and spiritually step outside of your problems. Over time, you find that doing so provides you with practical answers to difficult challenges.

There are no hard and fast rules about why you should make time for spiritual practices or what they should look like. Dedicate time to this area and use the time as you wish. You can certainly pray if you identify with a specific religion, but other practices can contribute to a stronger sense of spiritual connection. Sitting in silence or nature can be just as powerful as opening up a religious text. You can use fossilized stones, animal totems, or artwork that feels meaningful.

Embracing a spiritual practice has the power to change the entire trajectory of your life. You will feel supported by more than your individual body and mind, feeling more connected. Rich connections equate to a richer and fuller life. There isn't a wrong or a right way to approach spirituality. You can embrace traditional religion, or you can simply surround yourself with experiences that make you feel connected. Doing this is crucial for good self-care.